NEW JACOBINISM

Also by Claes G. Ryn

Will, Imagination and Reason

Democracy and the Ethical Life

Individualism and Community (in Swedish)

The New Conservatism in the United States (in Swedish)

Irving Babbitt in Our Time (co-editor)

THE NEW JACOBINISM

CAN DEMOCRACY SURVIVE?

CLAES G. RYN

NATIONAL HUMANITIES INSTITUTE

Washington, D.C.

Copyright © 1991 by the National Humanities Institute, Washington, D.C. All rights reserved. No part of this publication may be used or reproduced in any manner without permission in writing from the National Humanities Institute except in the case of brief quotations in books, articles, or reviews.

Library of Congress Catalog Number: 91-2774
ISBN: 0-932783-03-1
Printed in the United States of America

Library of Congress Cataloging-in-Publication Data

Ryn, Claes G., 1943-
    The new Jacobinism : can democracy survive? / Claes G. Ryn.
    p. cm.
    Includes bibliographical references and index.
    ISBN 0-932783-03-1
    1. Democracy. 2. Political ethics. 3. Political obligation. I. Title.
JC423.R96   1991   91-2774
321.8–dc20   CIP

The National Humanities Institute is a tax-exempt, educational and research organization that promotes significant research, publication, and teaching in the humanities, including the social sciences properly understood. It seeks to contribute to the reinvigoration and development of the principles upon which Western civilization is based.

Executive Committee

Claes G. Ryn
Chairman

Joseph Baldacchino
President

Russell Kirk
Treasurer

Board of Trustees

Hon. Richard Nixon
Honorary Chairman

Edward S. Babbitt, Jr.
President, Avatar Associates
New York, New York

William M. Benton
Chairman of the Board
Verimed Corporation
Fort Lauderdale, Florida

Dwight L. Chapin
Publisher
Weston, Connecticut

Mrs. Herbert Dow Doan
Midland, Michigan

Hon. Robert F. Ellsworth
President
Robert Ellsworth & Co., Inc.
Washington, D.C.

Sture Eskilsson
Chairman of the Board
Swedish Enterprise Foundation
Stockholm, Sweden

Rafael D. Pagán
Chairman – CEO
Pagán International
Washington, D.C.

Mrs. David A. Scott
Bethesda, Maryland

Academic Board

Russell Kirk
Chairman

John W. Aldridge
Professor of English
University of Michigan

Jude P. Dougherty
Dean, School of Philosophy
The Catholic University of America; Editor, The Review of Metaphysics

Paul Gottfried
Professor of Humanities
Elizabethtown College
Editor, This World

Forrest McDonald
Professor of History
University of Alabama

Robert A. Nisbet
Schweitzer Professor
Emeritus of the Humanities
Columbia University

George A. Panichas
Professor of English
University of Maryland
Editor, Modern Age

Peter J. Stanlis
Distinguished Professor
of Humanities Emeritus
Rockford College

NATIONAL HUMANITIES INSTITUTE
214 Massachusetts Avenue, N.E.
Suite 470
Washington, D.C. 20002
(202) 544-3158

Acknowledgments

This study was read in manuscript by Joseph Baldacchino, President of the National Humanities Institute, and James M. Miclot, David A. Scott Scholar in Political Theory at the Institute. I gratefully acknowledge their helpful suggestions.

CLAES G. RYN

Washington, D.C.
February 1991

Contents

Chapter One
Democracy and Jacobinism   9

Chapter Two
Conflicting Types of Democracy   19

Chapter Three
The Ethos of the Decentralized Society   25

Chapter Four
Democracy and Aristocratic Restraint   31

Chapter Five
Rousseau and Plebiscitary Conformity   39

Chapter Six
Patriotism, Nationalism, and
    Cosmopolitanism   45

Chapter Seven
Ethical Universality vs.
    Ethical Uniformity   49

Chapter Eight
The Decline of Democracy   55

Chapter Nine
The New Jacobins   67

Chapter Ten
Jacobinism and Capitalism   77

Chapter Eleven
Recovering Moral Realism   93

Index   97

I

Democracy and Jacobinism

Contrary to widespread belief, evidence is accumulating that Western democracy is in continuous and serious decline. Perhaps the most compelling sign of trouble is the complacency that marks most public discussion of democracy. Many commentators proclaim democracy's triumph over evil political forces in the world and hold up today's Western society as a model for all humanity. They do so in the face of glaring symptoms of social decay. The following brief list is merely suggestive: Political opportunism, demagoguery, and other irresponsibility, attitudes of self-indulgence and short-sightedness, the decline of the family, crime and other dishonesty, drug abuse, sexual promiscuity, academic shoddiness and ideologizing, religious superficiality and sentimentalism, crudity and debauchery in arts and entertainment – in their pervasiveness and virulence these and other phenomena indicate a disintegration of civilization. Yet, the problems of democracy are, if not ignored, at least discounted, evaded, or misunderstood. Some seriously entertain speculation that present-day Western society represents the culmination of mankind's historical struggle for enlightenment and well-being, that its ideas and institutions signal the end of history. This frantic self-praise suggests either a flight from reality or a cynical exploitation of moods of escapism. The celebration of democracy hangs like a narcotic cloud over the public, inducing an intellectual daze and spells of euphoria. No realistic assessment of the state of Western democracy is possible without cutting through the democratist fog.

The purpose here is to identify and analyze what may be democracy's central problem. Before some reflections can be presented regarding democracy's present condition in the West and its likely prospects, it is necessary to take up several closely connected philosophical issues. First of all, two different meanings of the term "democracy" need to be distinguished. One of the symptoms of democracy's precarious condition is the uncritical manner in which the word is used. In both theory and practice two radically different notions of popular government are blurred. Only one of these is compatible with liberty and civilized life. At a time when Eastern European countries are struggling free of Soviet domination and national identities are reaffirmed or shaped, the Western democracies, for all of their wealth and technological prowess, are setting examples of dubious value. They may be discrediting democracy in the eyes of more discriminating observers. Certain ethical considerations that are necessary to defining a civilized form of popular government are equally important to defining responsible nationhood.

Although the difficulties of Western democracy are manifold and have no single source, the most important can be seen as directly or indirectly induced by a deficiency at the ethical center. Democracy is suffering the consequences of an evasion of individual moral responsibility. The concrete and specific personal obligations of the here and now that were central to an older Western morality are being replaced by allegedly superior moral goals that are more abstract and distant. These goals concern generalized efforts on behalf of large aggregates of people. As the imagination is shaped by the needs of impersonal collectives, attention is distracted from the tasks actually facing the individual. Personal and concrete responsibilities begin to appear insignificant and trivial in comparison with great tasks to be performed by others far away. The burden of effort is shifted from individuals and local communities. As will be explained, the continual expansion and centralization of the modern democratic state can be seen in part as both manifesting and aggravating an erosion of personal responsibility. A few basic distinctions and definitions will make it easier to discern the extent and import of the problems of present-day Western democracy. They will also make it possible to recognize the questionable nature of some current efforts to shore up democracy by making it more "virtuous" and more ambitious abroad.

The profound problems of democracy show the effects of moral, cultural, and political tendencies that have long worked their influence in the Western world. Many of the phenomena that today threaten popular government can be traced back to sentiments and ideas that gained prominence in connection with the French Revolution that began in 1789. The vision of a new egalitarian order and of popular rule freed not only from traditional elites but from traditional moral and cultural restraints of all kinds had been formulated with great imaginative power by Jean-Jacques Rousseau a few decades earlier. Rousseau's notion of the natural goodness of man gave rise to a radical redefinition of moral virtue. It undermined the ancient belief that checks must be placed on individual and collective action and formed the basis for the idea that the popular majority of the moment should have unlimited sovereignty. In France the Rousseauistic vision of a new society was espoused with increasing militancy by the Jacobin clubs which saw themselves as incorruptible guardians of universal principles. The moral and ideological fervor of the Jacobins permeated the French Revolution. In its most uncompromising form Jacobinism helped inspire the revolution's hatred of traditional elites, its reign of terror, and its messianic ambitions.[1]

The Jacobin spirit has long been balanced and moderated in the Western world by various countervailing influences. Within today's Western democracies what may be termed a new Jacobinism is working to sever the remaining connections between popular government and the traditional Western view of man and society. It employs a somewhat different idiom than the earlier Jacobinism and incorporates various new ingredients, but it is essentially continuous with the old urge to replace historically evolved societies with an egalitarian order. The new Jacobinism is much in evidence in present efforts to turn democracy into a world-wide moral crusade. A sign of its influence is that it is well represented across the political-intellectual spectrum. Paradoxically, it often finds expression even among people called "conservatives."

Because of the spread of radical attitudes in academia, publishing, journalism, religion, the arts, and other fields, many people with a lingering attachment to the old Western tradition shrink from affirming it in ways that may be offensive to the dominant trend. Really to chal-

---

1. On the French Jacobins, see Simon Schama, *Citizens* (New York: Knopf, 1989), a detailed and richly evocative chronicle of the French Revolution, and Michael Kennedy, *The Jacobin Clubs in the French Revolution* (Princeton: Princeton University Press, 1982).

lenge the moral and intellectual powers in the ascendant is to place one's career in jeopardy and to risk losing the rewards that come from being in tune with the times. To the extent that the old but disapproved beliefs are not hidden or given up, means are found by those holding them to present them in ways more pleasing to the *Zeitgeist*. In fact, the old beliefs undergo a subtle change. They are discovered to be not quite so distant from the favored opinions of the day as once thought. Fear and opportunism join forces. Many cooperate in this self-deluding work of attunement to the new order. One result is that today ideas are sometimes presented as a defense of the Western tradition that are actually radical reinterpretations of that tradition. In this manner the *Zeitgeist* co-opts what it does not openly destroy.

The new Jacobinism is not a movement with settled boundaries, definite membership, or precise ideological definition. No single contemporary source provides a standard of orthodoxy. The new Jacobinism manifests itself in many fields – political, intellectual, and aesthetical. It influences people differently and in different degrees. Often it is mixed in particular persons with ideas and personality traits that have other origins. And yet where the new Jacobinism is present it has its own discernible tenor and moral-intellectual momentum and direction. The name here chosen to describe it points to a striking resemblance to an older form of missionary zeal, one that profoundly changed the Western world and permanently affected mankind as a whole. More than any other figure of the past, Rousseau may embody the moral and intellectual stance in which the Jacobin spirit finds its purest expression.

This book will make no systematic effort to classify individuals as representatives of the new Jacobinism. Nor will it attempt any comprehensive analysis and assessment of particular writers. The book aims to identify, illustrate, and analyze a general phenomenon, a tendency of thought, imagination, and action that need not be, indeed, rarely is, the whole truth about any particular person.

The following chapters provide some broad distinctions and definitions that are intended to clarify the condition of Western democracy and explain the seriousness of the crisis in which it finds itself. The new Jacobinism can be seen as a common denominator, an organizing and structuring force in the stream of ideas, sentiments, and practice that is transforming Western society.

This book will frequently compare Jacobinism with that against which it rebels. It will be contrasted with what can conveniently be summarized as "the Western heritage," "traditional society," "the old ethos," or the like. It should be made clear at the outset, and underlined, that this phraseology is not meant to imply that the choice facing today's Westerners is between a Jacobin break with the ancient Western civilization inspired by Greece, Rome, and Christianity and a return to the ideas and practices of the past.

That the past cannot simply be repeated hardly needs proving. Any revitalization or recovery of the Western traditions today must be a rearticulation of old insights and values in new circumstances. It requires a full and sensitive consideration of the best that has been put forth by Western modernity and the incorporation of those elements into the ancient heritage. A continuation of the Western traditions must of necessity be a development and reconstitution of earlier achievements. Even in historical periods of relative stability and continuity the words of Edmund Burke apply: "A state without the means of some change is without the means of its conservation." In a healthy civilization old and new must blend and shape each other. "The whole, at one time, is never old or middle-aged or young, but, in a condition of unchangeable constancy, moves on through the varied tenor of perpetual decay, fall, renovation, and progression." [2] Civilization, if it is to maintain itself, cannot be the mere imitation or repetition of old patterns. It must be a fresh, vital force in the present. Tradition degenerates into deadening routine and antiquarian, merely formal traditionalism unless it comes alive in the here and now through the

---

2. Edmund Burke, *Reflections on the Revolution in France* (Indianapolis: Hackett Publishing Company, 1987), 19, 35.

creativity of individuals who know both humanity's past and its new circumstances.

Because of the success of the attacks on traditional Western civilization, many people who grieve its destruction and are reluctant to adjust to what seems an ever more extreme and perverse "modernity" are tempted to escape from the realities of the present. They retreat into feelings of suffering purity and withdraw into the catacombs, as it were. The great "tradition" becomes a buried treasure of the past to be held in safe-keeping for coming generations. Considering the severity of the problems of the Western world, such attitudes of resignation should perhaps not be judged too harshly. But the many references in this book to the conflict between Jacobinism and Western civilization are not intended to suggest that the kind of society that forms the alternative to a Jacobin vision has its definition somewhere in the past. It is assumed, on the contrary, that insofar as traditional Western society can still be carried forward, it must be done through the kind of revitalization and reconstruction of civilization that was described earlier. Indeed, some of the terms that express Jacobin ideas – "democracy," "equality," etc. – have different meanings which, although alien to Jacobinism, grow out of distinctly modern considerations stressed also by the Jacobins. Modernity, including the French Revolution, contains opposed potentialities. Some of these can be reconciled with the older Western view of man and society and may even be indispensable to its reinvigoration and development. Other potentialities of modernity, such as those found most appealing by the Jacobin spirit, manifest a sharp, often hate-driven break with the ancient ways of the West. Thus it should be kept in mind that the tension ultimately of concern in this book is not between old and new but between those ideas and practices of the modern world that have actual or potential continuity with the ancient heritage of humane civilization and those that serve to destroy it.

One reason why Jacobinism has been able to do much damage to the ethical and cultural foundations of popular government is that obviously there are some good grounds for having reservations about the old Western tradition. Even its admirers recognize flaws and the need for remedies. At least some of the problems raised by the Jacobins and addressed by them in a radical, uncompromising way are real problems, although they can be understood and dealt with in a very different manner. The intellectual and moral confusion of the West has obscured the broad range of possible motives for desiring change. It is essential to be able to separate between attempts to gut or obliterate old traditions and constructive efforts to revise and develop them. Seemingly small and subtle differences in terminology or meaning can have large significance. Hence the emphasis in this book on distinctions, contrasts, and definitions.

II

Conflicting Types of Democracy

The distinction between two different forms of popular government has been set forth at length elsewhere.[1] Here it can only be summarized. Although both notions of government are referred to as "democracy," they are not different versions of the same kind of government. They imply radically different understandings of human nature and society and have radically different institutional entailments. They are ultimately incompatible. The one may be called constitutional or representative democracy, the other plebiscitary or majoritarian democracy. The former is closely related to the old Western view of man's

---

1. See Claes G. Ryn, *Democracy and the Ethical Life*, 2nd expanded ed. (Washington, D.C.: The Catholic University of America Press, 1990).

moral predicament. The latter flows from the kinds of ideas advocated by Rousseau and the Jacobins. Constitutional democracy consists of popular rule under self-imposed restraints and representative, decentralized institutions. Its aim is not to enact the popular wishes of the moment but to articulate what in American constitutional parlance is called the deliberate sense of the people. Plebiscitary democracy aspires to rule according to the popular majority of the moment. To ensure the speediest possible implementation of their wishes it seeks the removal of representative, decentralized and decentralizing practices and structures that limit the power of the numerical majority. Plebiscitary democrats recognize that, especially in large modern societies, the people need government officials to serve them, but the proper role of these officials is not to exercise independent judgment in the determination of the public interest. They should be agents of the majority.

Constitutional democracy assumes a human nature divided between higher and lower potentialities and sees a need to guard against merely self-serving, imprudent, and even tyrannical impulses in the individual and the people as a whole. In a constitutional democracy the people and their representatives adopt restraints on power to arm themselves in advance against their own moments of weakness and short-sightedness. In awareness of the flaws of human nature, they do not wish to be governed according to their own impulse of the moment. Sound government requires that the popular opinions of the moment be carefully scrutinized, sometimes that they be resisted by responsible leaders. The real, more enduring will of the people emerges over time through the interplay between popular opinion, as expressed in elections and public debate, and the informed, independent judgment of popular representatives.

But plebiscitary democracy does not entertain any deep-seated suspicions regarding human nature. The wishes of the majority at any particular time are regarded as the best expression of the will of the people. That will should become public policy without delay. If the people need leadership, it is of a kind that tries to anticipate not yet fully formed popular desires in order to speed their enactment.

The two conceptions of democracy entail sharply different understandings of what constitutes a society and a people. Constitutional democracy assumes a decentralized society in which the lives of most citizens are centered in small, chiefly private, and local associations, what Robert Nisbet calls autonomous groups. There are many centers and levels of power. Political authority is widely dispersed, enabling regional and local entities to exercise real independence. American federalism and American tradition in general exemplify the decentralized socio-political structures of constitutional democracy. In such a society the citizens participate in and are shaped by communal relations that are concrete, specific, and local. They tend to define their own interests not as discrete individuals but as members of the groups they most treasure, starting with the family and other associations at close range. By the "people" constitutional democracy does not understand an undifferentiated mass of individuals, whose will could be obtained by simply counting up the votes according to the formula one-man-one-vote. This numerical method disregards the social and qualitative ties between individuals. It ignores the fact that the people express their humanity and find their deepest satisfaction in associations of various kinds and that their interests as members of social subdivisions deserve consideration. Constitutional popular rule recognizes the need to adjust government structures and elections to a proliferation and diversity of interests and particular circumstances.

Plebiscitary democracy takes the politically most significant meaning of "the people" to be the undifferentiated mass of individuals. Government should serve the national majority, whose will is ascertained by numerical, merely quantitative methods. Fifty per cent plus one should rule. The measure of good democracy is that the popular majority have effective control over public policy. Regional and local interests are wholly subordinated to the majority of the most comprehensive political entity. The political dynamic of plebiscitary democracy is to mobilize, expand, and centralize government. The effect is to erode local and private autonomy and initiative and to efface what is locally and regionally distinctive.

It needs to be added that the dichotomy between two ultimately incompatible forms of democracy is but a part of a more comprehensive dichotomy that takes account of incompatible views of human life. The significance of the contrast between constitutional and plebiscitary popular rule becomes clearer when that distinction is related to a number of analogous and closely related distinctions. Together, all of these distinctions elaborate different aspects of larger contending notions of man and society. Among the many terms that can be dichotomized in ways analogous to the dichotomy of the word "democracy" are "liberty," "capitalism," and "free market." Dichotomies of these terms make explicit various meanings that lie implicit in the distinction between constitutional and plebiscitary democracy as well as in each of the other distinctions. As in the case of "democracy," great practical and theoretical confusion often hides behind the words "liberty," "capitalism," and "free market," each of which contains radically opposed potentialities. Like "democracy," the words have certain meanings that connect them to the Jacobin passion for overturning traditional societies.

III

The Ethos of the Decentralized Society

The decentralization that is characteristic of Western constitutional democracy reflects a particular understanding of human nature and morality. That understanding is deeply rooted in Christian ideas of community and virtue that are akin to earlier Greek ideas, especially those of Aristotle. The individual's primary moral responsibility is to make the best of self and to love neighbor. This is a demanding notion of virtue, for nothing is more difficult than overcoming one's own selfishness and behaving charitably toward people of flesh and blood at close range. People with names and faces have a way of presenting us with concrete and immediate obligations. Sometimes they make highly uncomfortable demands on our time and energy. To make charitable behavior even more difficult, they may be our competitors, perhaps also difficult and unlikable. Moral responsibility is achieved only slowly and with effort. It is in daily life, primarily in one's own intimate associations, that opportunities for love of neighbor are actually present. Man's moral character is shaped and tested first and foremost in relationships that are up close and personal.

Virtue manifested as love of neighbor may be contrasted with what is perhaps the most common modern idea of virtue. The latter lets individuals claim moral worth who show no particular signs of moral character in their actual conduct and who may, by traditional moral standards, actually be personally odious and very hard for people to live or work with. Their virtue is that they entertain benevolent sentiments for various abstract entities, such as "the people," "mankind," "the proletariat," "the poor," "the downtrodden," "the starving third world," or the like – categories that are all comfortably distant from the emoting person and which therefore impose no concrete and personally demanding obligations on the individual. Still, this sentimental posture of caring contains a pleasant ingredient of self-applause. It is, as it were, morality made easy. It presupposes no difficult improvement of self in actual human relationships.

Traditional Western morality creates a strong presumption that man's primary moral obligation is to deal with problems at close range, starting with self. The individual is acutely aware of his own weaknesses, aware that much needs to be done to remedy them. Doing well by family, kindred, friends, and colleagues is in itself a demanding task. If this task does not consume the energy of the individual, other heavy and pressing responsibilities await most human beings rather close to home and workplace. These should be attended to before presuming to tell people at a great distance how to live. We demonstrate our capacity for humanity in acts of character, and chiefly within the concrete relationships of daily life. This attitude has been a central feature of the ethos of the decentralized society. The people most immediately touched by problems or opportunities are thought to have the main responsibility for acting on them.

The presumption that much needs improving *here* before turning attention elsewhere has shaped a corresponding attitude toward international relations: a country's primary duty is to conduct its own affairs and repair its own flaws. An interest in neighboring countries and the rest of the world comes naturally to any civilized society; the benefits of contacts across borders are numerous and varied: commercial, cultural, political, and military. But the effect of the old morality of character is to build self-restraint and respect for others into these relationships and to reduce the danger of conflict. Ordinarily a country has no reason to interfere militarily or otherwise with other countries except to protect its own vital interests and defend itself against threats.

The consequences of the fading of the old moral ethos are profound and far-reaching. The modern substitution of a sentimental love of mankind for personal character has shifted the burden of moral responsibility away from individuals, groups, and local communities. Obligations have been transferred to government, which has expanded greatly and become highly centralized. It is now widely believed that a person demonstrates moral worth by wishing to order other people's lives according to allegedly benevolent political schemes. The stronger that wish, the greater the evidence of virtue. Domestically, this morality places people under the administrative supervision of government. Internationally, it provides a mandate for telling other countries what is good for them.

It is important to understand that the older ethos now being pushed back is no mere abstract idea or etherial sentiment. Whether it influences private, local, national, or international conduct it is a disposition of character that shapes individuals and socio-political structures in a wide range of concrete ways. Similarly, the weakening of that ethos has large and tangible consequences. The effects are not confined to certain parts of social life. Not only government but every other social institution and structure is transformed by the change. It is obvious that the meaning of "democracy" will be very different depending on the presence or absence of the older Western ethos. But the same is true, for example, of "the free market." Just as in government form and substance will vary with the personalities of those who make decisions, so in the marketplace the content of supply and demand, the manner of competition, and the organization of business will be different depending on the outlook and character of the persons who produce and consume.

IV

Democracy and Aristocratic Restraint

The view of human nature and morality that helps generate the decentralized, group-oriented society from which constitutional democracy is indistinguishable also fosters the kind of citizenship and leadership on which this government depends. Only people who are used to self-discipline and respect for others can sustain a form of government in which the citizens must accept the restraint of law and accommodate different interests. In a democracy the largest possible number of people are supposed to participate in governing. A person of bad character and other flaws is poorly equipped to rule self, to say nothing of influencing the lives of others by voting or holding office. High morality cannot be expected to set the tone in any society, but more than any other form of government a democracy is dependent for its success on a citizenry with standards of conduct above the ordinary. A democracy also stands in special need of leadership by people of proven character. According to the old Western view, responsible behavior gets its start at home and in nearby associations. A capacity for leadership may eventually be demonstrated in the wider local community. There the individual remains under rather close scrutiny. Potential leaders stand out partly as moral examples. In traditional Western society it was assumed that people worthy of special political influence would prove themselves in concrete action within their own sphere of life and work. They would have a good reputation built on long observation by peers. A responsible leader was known, not by repeated professions of high virtue, but by demonstrated integrity, modesty, and strength of will. Indeed, suspicions attached to individuals facile with noble phrases. Preferably, power should be given to people of moral substance and insight. The implication for democracy, where most people are to have a share in government, is that the special obligation to act responsibly must be widely accepted and encouraged.

Plato never contemplates the possibility of what is here called constitutional democracy. In the terms of the present discussion he only acknowledges the possibility of plebiscitary democracy. He associates democracy with undisciplined freedom. The soul of the democrat follows the whim of the moment. Democracy establishes equality of pleasures and of individuals. Those gain political power who most successfully pander to the popular impulse of the moment. For Plato democracy destroys the last vestiges of aristocratic moral and intellectual order and ushers in the brutal lawlessness of tyranny.

Constitutional democracy, by contrast, can be seen as an attempt to realize freedom under law by building aristocratic personality traits and other elements into popular government. It does so by encouraging and drawing upon self-control among citizens in general and upon the social structures that this discipline engenders. Political institutions and processes are deliberately shaped in ways that increase the likelihood that persons of character and wisdom will be influential. The original American Constitution provides many examples of an effort to counteract such dangers of plebiscitarianism as demagoguery and rabble-rousing, what the Framers scorn as "democracy." Not only does the Constitution give no power whatever to a numerical national majority, the American people have political standing *only* as members of political subdivisions. The Constitution also places various checks on the authority it does grant to the people. Popular opinion is sifted through representative institutions. In the words of Federalist No. 10, it is desirable "to refine and enlarge the public views by passing them through the medium of a chosen body of citizens, whose wisdom may best discern the true interest of their country." [1] The Framers also assumed that voting would be restricted to individuals who, as property holders, were expected to act more responsibly than others. To increase the odds of well-informed, responsible decisions the Framers deliberately shielded many office holders from the pressures of popular opinion. Senators and Presidents would be elected only indirectly by the people. They would also have fairly substantial terms of office, making it easier for them to follow their own best judgment. Members of the Supreme Court would be even further removed from popular pressures. The task of selecting a president was placed in the hands of the Electoral College. This body was intended to consist of experienced individuals capable of distinguishing between presidential contenders of integrity and ability and ones of questionable character and ambition.

A similar prejudice against rash, partisan, or uninformed opinion would be manifested in State and local checks on political power and in social institutions generally. For a long time the American people sanctioned aristocratic or quasi-aristocratic self-limitations as appropriate to articulating and promoting their own enduring will.

---

1. Hamilton, Madison, and Jay, *The Federalist Papers*, ed. Clinton Rossiter (New York: New American Library, 1961), No. 10 (Madison), 82.

The Framers of America's political institutions were thus uninterested in plebiscitary rule. To the extent that they considered it at all, it was to warn against its dangers. Among the influences that shaped their anti-plebiscitary views were a distinctive and concrete colonial experience permeated by religious faith, a tradition of localism, and the particularities of the historically rooted common law.[2] Although alien to the Framers, plebiscitarianism has had its American defenders, and it has gained much ground over time. Traditional political institutions have been transformed by changing practice and by constitutional amendment and interpretation. They have also come under mounting intellectual assault. Some critics who do not wish to appear hostile to the work of the Framers reinterpret "the Founding" as being far more majoritarian and egalitarian than previously thought. Others reject traditional institutions outright as being "elitist" and inimical to real popular rule.

At the same time that plebiscitary sentiments restructure America's political and social institutions, the extent of the change is obscured by philosophical confusion. The failure to make the

---

2. For a discussion of the moral, intellectual, and cultural roots of the American Framers, see Forrest McDonald, *Novus Ordo Seclorum: The Intellectual Origins of the Constitution* (Lawrence, Kansas: University Press of Kansas, 1985) and Russell Kirk, *The Conservative Constitution* (Washington, D.C.: Regnery Gateway, 1990).

all-important distinction between constitutional and plebiscitary popular rule results in an inability to see how much is really at stake.

It should be remembered that government is indistinguishable from moral, intellectual, and cultural conditions that give it shape and direction, that it manifests the preferences of an entire civilization. The transformation of American political practice and theory forms part of developments that encompass social life as a whole. If the weakening of ethical and other restraint is changing American government, so is it changing intellectual, cultural, and economic life. It is appropriate to reiterate that the distinction between two forms of popular government, one compatible and one incompatible with aristocratic self-discipline, implies other distinctions between opposed potentialities of human life. Again, terms like "liberty," "private property," or "free market," have to be dichotomized no less than "democracy." Central to the needed dichotomies is the extent to which particular understandings emphasize or deemphasize the importance of ethical and other restraints and the kind of social and political structures from which they are indistinguishable. Each of the terms can have vastly different meanings. Without the proper distinctions, it is not possible meaningfully to classify advocates of "liberty," "private property," or "the free market." Like "democracy," these terms may hide meanings that are sharply at odds with the old Western ethical and cultural ethos and may actually express a burning wish to overturn traditional society. The extent of the transformation of America and of the larger civilization to which it belongs is partly hidden by the vague and uncritical use of general terms.

V

Rousseau and Plebiscitary Conformity

If traditional American constitutional government answers roughly to the idea of constitutional popular rule, the idea of plebiscitary democracy is advocated in its purest form by Jean-Jacques Rousseau.[1] Starting from a belief in the natural goodness of man, Rousseau rejects the old belief that human nature needs moral and other restraints. Traditional civilization enslaves man to structures of inequality and other artificiality. By completely destroying the old society the people

---

1. For further substantiation of the following interpretation of Rousseau's ethical and political ideas, see the extensive analysis and critical assessment of Rousseau in Ryn, *Democracy*, esp. Chs. V-VIII. For a general interpretation of Rousseau and his influence, see Irving Babbitt's pioneering and brilliantly perceptive *Rousseau and Romanticism* (New Brunswick: Transaction Books, 1991).

can form a new community of equality and brotherhood. As natural inclinations are liberated in the people they develop a common will. What Rousseau calls the general will is to be expressed by the majority. Since this will is inherently good, it should be subject to no legal or other checks. Popular sovereignty must be unrestricted. The popular will of the moment must be a law unto itself. "Yesterday's law is not binding today," Rousseau writes.[2] He dismisses constitutional and legal limits on the majority. He also utterly rejects the idea that representatives should help articulate the popular will. While the people may wish to entrust the *execution* of their wishes to government officials, representation in the determination of the popular will is a usurpation of popular sovereignty.

The majoritarian democracy envisioned by Rousseau is based on complete political equality. All citizens must carry the same weight. There should be literally "one-man-one-vote." Partly to ensure that objective, society must not be made up of a multiplicity of groups and associations and have many centers and levels of power. To express its will the people must form an undifferentiated mass of individuals. "It is imperative that there should be no sectional associations in the state." [3] Subdivisions in the state are for Rousseau partisan interests that dilute the sovereignty

---

2. Jean-Jacques Rousseau, *The Social Contract* (Harmondsworth: Penguin Books, 1970), Bk. III, Ch. 11, 135.

3. *Ibid.*, Bk. II, Ch. 3, 73.

of the people and divert the citizens from the common good. For the virtuous general will to manifest itself each person must decide freely and autonomously for himself, which is impossible if sectional interests affect his consciousness. Rousseau is at the same time a radical individualist, who separates the individual from groups and associations, and a radical collectivist, who makes the undifferentiated whole of the state the sole context for virtuous political striving.

Rousseau's wish to free the current majority from all restrictions, to dissolve the people into a homogeneous mass, abolish decentralization, and remove representative institutions could not be in sharper contrast to American traditions of constitutionalism, federalism, localism, and representation. He is working out the socio-political entailments of a view of human nature that clashes fundamentally with the view underlying constitutional democracy.

For Rousseau, the general will pronounced by the majority is the final political word. There is nothing above it to which the minority can appeal. The general will is itself the ultimate standard of political right. The minority is by definition wrong and should recognize its error. Not only is the minority not deserving of any protection, but if it persists in opposing the general will it must be forced to be free. There are no grounds for accommodating different interests. Political opinion divides between right and wrong, and there is no reason why wrong should be tolerated. Virtue is univocal, and power must be the monopoly of the majority. Rousseauistic political morality inspired the French Jacobins, *les vertueux* ("the virtuous"), with a sense of being agents of the people against vile conspiratorial forces. As the instrument of a new popular will in the making, Rousseau's ardent disciple Robespierre felt justified in crushing all opposition. Why should virtue not insist on total control? [4]

Rousseau's notion of virtuous power has important implications for international politics. He can be seen as one of the founders of modern nationalism. The general will is the will of a particular people and can tolerate no opposition. Since there can be no appeal to an authority beyond the general will, conflict between states is likely. Rousseau points out that "all peoples generate a kind of centrifugal force, by which they brush continuously against one another, and they all attempt to expand at the expense of their neighbors." [5] The weak may be swallowed up by the strong. Rousseau's thought has a marked militaristic bias. In the ancient Greek world his model is Sparta. For Rousseau the nationalistic impulse is closely connected with virtue. "Do we wish men to be virtuous," he asks. "Then let us

---

4. On Rousseauistic virtue as demanding uniformity, see Carol Blum, *Jean-Jacques Rousseau and the Republic of Virtue* (Ithaca: Cornell University Press, 1986). See also Ryn, *Democracy*, esp. Part Three.

5. Rousseau, *Social Contract*, Bk. II, Ch. 9, 92.

begin by making them love their country." "It is certain," he asserts, "that the greatest miracles of virtue have been produced by patriotism." [6] In his book on Poland Rousseau advocates instilling an ardent nationalism in the citizens. "The newly-born infant . . . must gaze upon the fatherland, and until his dying day should behold nothing else." [7] In the *Social Contract* Rousseau writes that the citizen should receive from the national collective "his life and being." [8]

---

6. Jean-Jacques Rousseau, *A Discourse on Political Economy* in *The Social Contract and Discourses* (New York: E.P. Dutton & Co., 1950), 301-302.

7. Jean-Jacques Rousseau, *The Government of Poland* (New York: Bobbs-Merrill, 1972), 19.

8. Rousseau, *Social Contract*, Bk. II, Ch. 7, 84.

VI

Patriotism, Nationalism, and Cosmopolitanism

It is here appropriate to extend the dichotomy between two sharply opposed forms of popular government to two very different ideas of nationhood. A distinction is needed between what may be called patriotism and nationalism. Selecting terms for particular meanings is always to some extent arbitrary. "Patriotism" and "nationalism" have no universally accepted definitions. The proposed distinction employs the terms in ways which may be at variance with some common usage.

The old morality of modesty and self-discipline, which is integral to constitutional democracy, does not preclude pride in personal strengths and accomplishments. Neither does it preclude local, regional, and national pride. But the patriotic celebration of national achievements does not signify the abandonment of a supranational moral norm. On the contrary, the standard for national self-regard is the same standard that judges the flaws of one's own people severely. The patriot is the first to feel shame and regret about unjust actions taken by his or her own country. Patriotism recognizes a standard beyond national prejudice and passion and maintains moral discrimination and self-control. While always ready to defend his own country against threats, the patriot is less prone to impose his will on other nations than to try to be an example for others. Just as in domestic politics the constitutional democrat is not insensitive to the possibly legitimate claims of various groups, so in international politics the patriot is not insensitive to the claims of other countries. Indeed, as one looking to improve the quality of life in his own country the patriot is receptive to the merits of other peoples and cultures and welcomes the variety of national customs as adding a spice to life.

Patriotism and cosmopolitanism, rightly understood, are compatible and complementary. The true cosmopolitan, like the patriot, is rooted in a particular cultural tradition but is to some extent at home in more than one country by virtue of the element of universality in his own particular background and in the traditions of other countries. The cosmopolitan and the patriot both recognize that the universal values of civilization can be realized in somewhat different ways depending on time and place. A sense of shared humanity and destiny keeps the patriot, even in war, considerate of competitors. Rarely in a conflict is all right on one side, and the present enemy is a possible future friend and ally.

Nationalism, by contrast, is an eruption of overweening ambition, a throwing off of individual and national self-control. Nationalism is self-absorbed and conceited, oblivious of the weaknesses of the country it champions. It is provincialism without the leaven of cosmopolitan breadth, disgression, and critical detachment. It recognizes no authority higher than its own national passion. It imagines itself as having a monopoly on right or as having a mission superseding moral norms. "My country, right or wrong." Nationalist politics is inherently intolerant, tyrannical, and expansionist.

Especially when offered without appropriate definitions, the idea that democracies are inherently peaceful and disinclined to aggression is so much nonsense. All depends on whether a particular democracy has the self-restraint that comes with character and civilized prejudices among its citizens and leaders. All depends on whether it is of the constitutional or plebiscitary type. Plebiscitary democracy aims to free the popular majority from checks on its prevailing will. In so doing it liberates also the desire for power and self-aggrandizement to which a people is sometimes prone and to which nationalist demagogues can appeal.

VII

Ethical Universality vs. Ethical Uniformity

Before attention is turned to the current state of constitutional democracy a few reflections on moral universality need to be added to the discussion of contrasting conceptions of popular rule and nationhood. Constitutional democracy assumes the need for moral restraint and discrimination on the part of the people and their leaders. With reference to what standard is this self-discipline to be exercised? Among those who profess a belief in moral universality it is common to understand the standard of right as a set of principles or precepts, discernible by reason, that exists apart from history and changing circumstances. In this perspective morality becomes the imitation of an abstract plan. But many features of constitutional democracy, shared to some extent with non-popular forms of government, suggest that it does not imply a static moral norm or model. Government by popular consent, a willingness to accommodate different interests, decentralization of authority, adjustment to circumstances, acceptance of diversity – these indicate that moral universality is better understood as something historically evolving. This does not mean that it lacks an enduring purpose but that changing and varying circumstances require creative and diverse articulations of the moral imperative.

The statesman can rely on no blueprint for the good society. Even the morally sensitive and responsible person is rarely certain beyond any doubt of what, specifically, is morally required in particular situations. It is ordinarily easier to identify what in self and others is clearly incompatible with the common good. An important objective of constitutional government is to hold back the more blatantly self-serving desires. It should be noted, however, that intentions that are not censured are provisionally judged to be compatible with the purpose of good and are allowed to pass into action. Concrete and specific aims are thereby enacted. To become a real power in human life, morality must be embodied, not imitated, in historical actions. These must be adjusted to the special needs of time and place. The universal must be realized through the particular. Together and over time, morally permissible actions give substance to and build up a certain quality of human existence. This purposive structure is a tentative embodiment of the good life, although one forever subject to reassessment and revision by morally sensitive human beings. Through a process of censure and qualified approval of particular intentions, moral civilization gradually evolves. Progress is never automatic or inevitable; moral decline and disaster always threaten. Such advance as lies within human capacity depends entirely on whether those who live at a particular time shoulder or shirk their individual moral responsibility.

Moral insight and guidance cannot be the monopoly of any single individual or group. Because of the complexity and diversity of human life, moral good must be advanced in a multiplicity of different ways that are adjusted to particular situations. No person, however enlightened and noble, can specify and encompass the needs of a whole society. Most human beings have some potential for contributing in their different capacities and special circumstances to the continuing articulation of moral good. Universality is not the same as uniformity. Many different interests have legitimate claims that are compatible with the common good. The universal does not abolish diversity. It harmonizes diversity. The universal blends with the uniqueness of countless personalities and causes, letting these enrich the larger harmony of the good life. It enlists them in its own cause by censuring whatever is merely idiosyncratic and destructive of moral community.

The phrase *e pluribus unum*, which sums up the achievement of the American Framers, does not signify the obliteration of diversity for the sake of unity. It signifies the harmonization of many different interests through proper self-restraint, both individual and institutional. Precisely because constitutional democracy cherishes diversity and decentralization of authority, it stands in special need of the moral self-control and discrimination that make pluralism and freedom civilizing forces and keep them from deteriorating into viciously factional conflict. In the ethical life particularity and universality are inseparable.

This notion of moral universality clashes head-on with the Rousseauistic idea that virtuous politics abjures particular interests and social subdivisions. Since in Rousseau's majoritarian democracy all right is found on one side, there is no reason to tolerate diversity.

A similar hostility to or suspicion of particular interests stems from the more intellectualistic conception that morality has its true standard in a rational norm existing apart from history. This moral abstractionism does not recognize the possibility formulated above – that it is by expressing itself through historical particularity and change that universality becomes a vital force in human life. The implications of denying the potential union of universality and particularity are stark and highly problematic. If political right is indeed adherence to a moral blueprint, personal freedom and social pluralism are, in the end, irrelevant to defining the common good. They should be tolerated, if at all, only as prescribed by the plan. No room need be left for improvisation and new discoveries. The common good would be best served if those who know the specifics of political right were in a position to dictate to others, which would minimize the incidence of distractions.

VIII

The Decline of Democracy

The preceding philosophical discussion of issues of ethics and politics has concrete applications to the state of modern Western society. It is time to turn to the problems facing democracy. The scope and seriousness of those problems could be illustrated by a very long list of examples. Only some of them will be highlighted that are particularly indicative of Western society's simultaneous slide into factionalism and plebiscitarianism. Most of the examples will be taken from the world's leading democracy, but the cited phenomena have their counterparts all over the Western world.

The gradual disappearance from Western society of the type of moral self-control and discrimination on which constitutional democracy depends has produced increasingly blatant partisanship and general socio-political fragmentation. The law, once regarded as an attempt to transcend mere power politics, is perceived more and more by lawmakers and voters alike as an instrument of partisan ambition, as a way of compelling the obedience of others, or, if existing law is opposed to one's own immediate interest, as an obstacle to be removed. The way in which the U.S. Constitution is widely viewed is a case in point.

A general decline of moral and cultural standards, accompanied by intensifying plebiscitary pressures, has gradually robbed American representative and other institutions of their aristocratic, restraining function and made the electorate less accepting of such leadership. Since 1913 the U.S. Senate has been elected by direct popular vote, and, despite the six-year term of its members, it has become, like other representative institutions, very sensitive to the opinions of the mass media and the general public. The selection of the President by the Electoral College is a formality. Today candidates for the presidency are especially subject to the vagaries of popular opinion and mass communication.

With the deterioration of the institutional supports for critical detachment and deliberation, responsible decision-making has become increasingly difficult. Among elected officials thought of the next election is pervasive. In political debate statements are made primarily with a view to some political advantage. Rare is the politician who would risk unpopularity or media censure by stating uncomfortable truths. Successful politicians tend to be individuals lacking in deeper insight and conviction. The need to appeal to the great mass of people on virtually all issues pushes political discussion to ever lower levels of sloganeering and pandering. Elections become embarrassing displays of simplistic demagoguery in which advertising and media consultants play central roles. Judged by the appeals made to voters, the public is assumed to have a simplistic, almost infantile view of the world.

At the same time, modern welfare politics and a long series of Supreme Court decisions have centralized American government and undermined state and local autonomy. The people vote in elections as before, but increasingly their sentiments are shaped and mobilized by people far away who can decide what issues are important and define the terms in which they should be discussed. Great power of this type has been accumulated at the national centers of politics and communication. Subjects that are distant and abstract are pushed into the forefront and draw attention away from tasks that are near and concrete.

Centralization of power coexists with attitudes of self-indulgence. That this should be the case is explained by the earlier discussion of virtue. The practice of personal, up-close responsibility that both manifests and builds character also buttresses localism and decentralization. Conversely, abdication of this kind of responsibility in favor of "great causes" ushers in a centralization of power. A listing of examples of declining personal initiative and self-discipline is at the same time a listing of phenomena that undermine decentralized social and political structures.

Lawlessness and permissiveness are common. Crime is epidemic. In many areas government lacks the ability or will to control it. What was long considered the fundamental responsibility of government, protecting the lives, limbs, and property of the citizens, is exercised erratically. There is a general hesitancy about enforcing standards. Doubts about the moral culpability of criminals and a reluctance to punish dissolves the line between criminals and non-criminals. In his description of democracy's lack of moral structure and drift toward tyranny, Plato says, "Isn't there something rather charming about the good-temper of those who have been sentenced in court? You must have noticed that in a democracy men sentenced to death or exile stay on, none the less, and go about among their fellows." [1] In the United States, justice has become so wrapped up in legalistic formalism that the question of substantive guilt or innocence frequently seems secondary.

Instances of fading self-discipline are prominent in all aspects of social life. Drug abuse is rampant. Sexual promiscuity is so common as to

---

1. Plato, *Republic* (Harmondsworth: Penguin Books, 1974), Bk. XIII, 558a, 376.

be considered almost normal and causes epidemics of venereal disease and AIDS. Abortions are performed in staggering numbers as a form of birth-control. The family is losing its cohesion and plays a much reduced role as transmitter of civilized values. Standards of personal behavior and deportment are falling. Old-fashioned honesty and integrity yield to shadiness and opportunism. Carelessness pushes out good workmanship. Commercialism is more and more obtrusive. Spending for consumption through borrowing is the order of the day both for individuals and government. The continual and substantial inflationary erosion of the currency, which sometimes halves its value in just a few years, shows the opportunism and cynicism of vote-buying politicians and the complicity of self-indulgent voters who want benefits without paying for them. In education standards are low, and the ideological fads and nostrums of the day replace attention to the insights and achievements of the ages. At the same time, diversions from real problems and responsibilities are everywhere. Entertainment forms an increasingly prominent part of Western culture and plays a central role in breaking down lingering traditional tastes and inhibitions. In the arts, the incidence of the crude, the ugly, and the offensive illustrates a collapse of aesthetical judgment. The churches try to avoid the subjects of individual sin, repentance, and character and offer a largely sentimental message of "love" and "compassion." Old distinctions between what is morally admirable and deplorable are radically challenged. Behaviors are accepted or held up for emulation that once were considered abhorrent. Again, Plato's comments about democracy's self-destruction come to mind: Voices appear in the decadent society and individual soul that "call insolence good breeding, license liberty, and shamelessness courage." [2]

The evidence of decline in today's Western democracies could be balanced against more encouraging signs, but these cannot remove the impression that a civilization is disintegrating, and not just at the periphery – but at its moral core. That core is the self-restraint and the particularized down-to-earth striving of individuals who try to make the best of themselves and the actual opportunities of their own lives. Social tension is reduced and community made possible in so far as society's members discipline their partisan ego and treat others with respect. Today, a moral flabbiness permits flight from real, up-close problems and opportunities into moral posturing. While high-sounding and ambitious goals are professed, social conflict intensifies.

To a growing extent political competition and social life in general have the characteristics of civil war by non-violent means. Constitutional and other legal restraints do have a formal existence still and even a fragile substantive efficacy, but more and more Western democracy exhibits the

---

2. *Ibid.*, Bk. 560e, 380.

dynamics of plebiscitary, majoritarian pressure politics.

Politics always has an element of raw conflict. In all societies order is derived in part from the threat of violence and other sanctions available to constituted authority. Another source of order is the enlightened self-interest of competing individuals and groups which leads them to recognize the utility of limiting their assertiveness. Constitutional democracy, too, relies on these sources of political cohesion. But more than any other form of government it needs a special self-control beyond the clever, calculating self-restraint of sophisticated egotism.[3] In this respect constitutional democracy is more demanding than any other form of government. It cannot function without considerable moral and general culture among its leaders and people. Erosion of the sense of moral common good may not immediately destroy enlightened self-interest in every sense; for a time even blatantly partisan groups may recognize the advantage of putting checks on their self-seeking. In a majoritarian system it is prudent, after all, to try to gain some wider acceptance. But partisanship unbounded by respect for what lies beyond private advantage becomes ever more grasping and aggressive.

Modern Western democracy displays two tendencies which might appear unrelated and even opposed to each other but which are actually different manifestations of the same break-up of

---

3. See Ryn, *Democracy*, esp. 20-26, 166-181.

moral community. One is the already mentioned fragmentation of society. This problem of political order is sometimes analyzed in terms of value relativism, nihilism, or liberal pluralism. The second tendency is the enormous and continuing expansion and centralization of government and of the educational, business, and media establishments that are closely intertwined with government.

Superficially regarded, what has here been called social fragmentation might seem to be just the kind of decentralized and group-oriented socio-political dynamic that was earlier said to be integral to constitutional democracy. Is not fragmentation the result of abandoning a definite and universal standard for the good society and tolerating a proliferation of particular interests? But it is necessary to consider the contrast between interests that are and interests that are not disciplined and harmonized with reference to a common ethical center. Social fragmentation is the term for the self-assertion of groups and individuals that recognize no obligation beyond their partisan causes and that are therefore approaching each other as belligerents. In the absence of respect for a universal good, the particular group can never form a genuine community. It is merely an aggregate of ego-centered interests and is itself threatened internally by conflict and disintegration. The more numerous are such self-seeking associations and individuals, the greater is society's element of moral fragmentation. Groups that do achieve real community internally by transcending the merely private interests of their members thereby also find a common ground with other similarly motivated groups and come to share with them in the ethical life of the larger society. Again, moral universality does not abolish particularity. It expresses itself in diverse concrete shapes in response to the needs of circumstance. Groups and individuals that pursue their special aspirations while recognizing the legitimacy of other interests and while adjusting to what lies above pure partisanship become the particularized embodiments of universality and move society toward the ethical center. To that extent groups and individuals form unity in diversity and build up the common good.

Even in the best of societies groups will range in moral quality from the praiseworthy to the deplorable. The civilized society will seek ways to encourage the former and restrict the latter. Constitutional and other formative structures are here important. Groups are everywhere prone to disregard the rightful claims of others, and their self-absorption can threaten social order. Because of the wide latitude that constitutional democracy grants groups and individuals to pursue their interests, that form of government more than any other needs a citizenry that is capable of self-restraint. Some externally imposed limitations on freedom are always necessary, but if the self-imposed limitations of groups and individuals are widely and greatly weakened, the constitutional system is itself in jeopardy. In today's Western democracies partisanship divorced from considerations of the common good is rampant – hence the appropriateness of the term fragmentation.

Regarding the second-mentioned tendency, the dramatic growth of central power, Robert Nisbet has demonstrated that the modern administrative state is both cause and consequence of the deterioration of the older decentralized and community-oriented Western society.[4] Centralized bureaucracies have gathered unto themselves power taken from or yielded by regional, local, and private authority. The kind of internal, diversified cohesion that evolved from the old Western ethos is being replaced by an externally and centrally imposed order. Of the particular historical forces that have greatly aided the accumulation and centralization of government power Nisbet attaches much importance to military mobilization in behalf of internationalist ideological causes.

The fragmentation and the centralization of power are both forms of the abandonment of the old notion of community through self-control. They are both examples of the partisan pursuit of power at the expense of competing interests. The burgeoning bureaucratic-administrative state replaces the relative autonomy and mutual accommodation of a wide variety of interests with

---

4. See, in particular, Robert Nisbet, *The Quest for Community* (San Francisco: Institute for Contemporary Studies, 1990).

unified control. Although government elites claim to be above partisanship and often invoke moral principle, their high-sounding language virtually always sanctions an expansion, rarely a reduction, of their own centralized power.

Plato cites variety, movement, and color as attributes of democracy. Having adopted the silly and destructive assumption that all individuals and preferences have equal claim to attention, democracy exhibits a measure of tolerance as it caters to the whim of the moment. Though certainly not without application to today's Western democracies, Plato's comment regarding freedom and diversity in democracy is contradicted by another and increasingly prominent feature of today's Western societies, their element of conformity and thought-control. Through government, mass media, education, and entertainment a plebiscitary, democratist orthodoxy is promulgated and enforced which changes somewhat depending upon the fortunes of particular pressure groups. Violation of its tenets is grounds for grave suspicions about the offender and cause for ostracization, or worse. Professions of liberal tolerance and free speech somehow interfere not at all with the enforcement of ideological assent. Describing these democratist doctrines in their most recent form is beyond the scope of this study. Suffice it to say that they lie opposite the views that people keep to themselves or express only in whispered conversation while looking anxiously over their shoulder to see who is listening. The vigilance and moralistic righteousness of those who watch over adherence to the prescribed democratist views and behaviors call to mind the French Jacobins. De Tocqueville comes closer than Plato to capturing this feature of modern democracy in his warnings about "soft" democratic despotism. Unlike older, non-democratic despotism, de Tocqueville writes, the new despotism "would degrade men without tormenting them."[5] Perhaps it is more appropriately said that today's democracy has invented a new form of torture.

---

5. Alexis de Tocqueville, *Democracy in America* (New Rochelle: Arlington House, undated), Fourth Book, Ch. VI, 336.

IX

The New Jacobins

There are signs that with the fading of the ethos of constitutionalism democratic despotism could turn less "soft." Individuals who find sources of personal power in the present state of democracy may become more ambitious and aggressive. They can draw for justification upon an already influential democratist ideology that invests democracy with a noble and world-wide mission. This ideology rejects what it calls moral relativism and claims to represent timeless and universal principles that should everywhere prevail. Since these principles are in substantial, if not unqualified, agreement with the beliefs of today's democracy, a new moral legitimacy is conferred upon it. The diligent promotion of these principles is seen as the way to overcome social fragmentation. Replacing diversity with unity is for many today an appealing vision. So is national assertiveness abroad in behalf of allegedly universal principles. Many speak and act as if the virtuous course is to impose an artificial, external order of principles on a disintegrating society while giving that society a moral mission beyond its borders. The moralistic language often masks strong political ambitions.

Among those who advocate a morally unified and internationally ambitious democracy it is common to draw prestige to their own preferences by ascribing them to various historical figures of moral and intellectual stature. Often a loosely defined "Western tradition" is invoked. Various of its great books are reinterpreted as offering support for the cause. Even thinkers like Plato and Aristotle, whose ideas might appear to have little or nothing in common with modern democratism, are used to boost its reputation. So are the Framers of the U.S. Constitution. The Framers are said to be enacting the ideas of others, John Locke prominent among them, who are interpreted with emphasis on the egalitarian strains within their thought. According to Allan Bloom, the American form of government recommends itself as the implementation of a moral plan. "Our story," he writes in glowing language, "is the majestic and triumphant march of freedom and equality." Bloom interprets "the American project" as advancing essentially the same plan as the French Revolution. Edmund Burke, the critic of the latter, sees arrogance and superficiality and great potential for tyranny in the idea that society should be made to conform to an abstract moral plan, but Bloom applauds that idea and attributes it to the Framers. For him the appeal of America is that it is a "great stage" on which the theories of philosophers and their students have been acted out. "There are almost no accidents." Bloom ascribes to the American Framers a wish, similar to Rousseau's, to phase out social diversity and particularity and to unify human beings in their common denominator. To recognize man's "natural rights," Bloom writes, is to have "a fundamental basis of unity and sameness." In America, he argues, people are asked "to give up 'their cultural individuality' and make themselves into that universal, abstract being who participates in natural rights." [1]

In Bloom's interpretation, the U.S. Framers are egalitarians and exponents of "majoritarianism." Like Rousseau, they are also disposed against a diversity of groups and interests. "For the Founders, minorities are in general bad things, mostly identical to factions, selfish groups who have no concern as such for the common good." Bloom's disparaging of social diversity and pluralism stems from a type of abstractionism that regards moral universality as separate from particularity. Like Rousseau, he associates politi-

---

1. Allan Bloom, *The Closing of the American Mind* (New York: Simon and Schuster, 1987), 97, 30-31. For an extensive analysis and assessment of Bloom's book, see Claes G. Ryn, "Universality or Uniformity?," *Modern Age*, Vol. 32, No. 1 (1988).

cal virtue with human sameness. Bloom describes the moral basis of the "American project" as follows: "Class, race, religion, national origin or culture all disappear or become dim when bathed in the light of natural rights, which give men common interests and make them truly brothers." [2] In Bloom's strained and even frivolous interpretation of the American Framers, they become virtually indistinguishable from the French Jacobins with their passion for spreading *liberté, égalité,* and *fraternité.*

Bloom's understanding of American principles is fairly typical of a spreading democratist ideology. This ideology shares essential features with the thought of Jean-Jacques Rousseau, the quintessential plebiscitarian. It is fittingly called the new Jacobinism. This ideology does not agree with contemporary Western democracy in all particulars, but neither does it offer much support for constitutional democracy as here understood. That its representatives sometimes invoke Locke does not change the picture, for it is a Locke that is not dissimilar to Rousseau. Louis Hartz once pointed to the Locke in question: "Locke has a hidden conformitarian germ to begin with, since natural law tells equal people equal things." [3] The

---

2. *Ibid.*, 31, 27. Bloom wants an exception to society's majoritarian regime in the universities, where the insightful should guide disciples toward enlightenment.

3. Louis Hartz, *The Liberal Tradition in America* (New York: Harcourt, Brace, Jovanovich, 1955), 11.

ideas of Bloom and others like him have far more in common with such figures from America's past as Thomas Paine and Thomas Jefferson, who had strong egalitarian and plebiscitary leanings, than with the authors of the U.S. Constitution.

What is often offered as a moral tonic for America thus includes a Jacobin passion for equality and virtuous unity that is likely to add to the push for uniformity and central control. The new Jacobinism buttresses the pressures to conform with a kind of moral rigorism. The belief that political virtue is summed up in specific "principles" or "rights" and that these are also best known by an intellectual elite with special powers of discernment breeds not only arrogance in those who consider themselves in the know but intolerance of those who deviate from the presumed moral prescriptions. Why, indeed, should the complexity and messiness of society not yield to the direction of the virtuous?

The potential for tyranny in this moral abstractionism is apparent, for example, in the attacks on historical thinking by many of its intellectual exponents. The belief that human life is inescapably historical and that the pursuit of good must be adjusted to time and place is rejected as a threat to moral universality and rectitude. To think of moral universality as affected by historical circumstance is, so it is asserted, to dissolve moral universality; a real moral standard must exist apart from the historical phenomena for which it is to be the standard. Besides revealing philosophically rather amateurish habits, this advocacy of a historically pure moral vantage point discloses the grounds for denying to individuality, particularity, and diversity as such any moral legitimacy. Let pure virtue rule! [4]

At a time of socio-political disintegration the new Jacobinism offers the prospect of moral politics. It plants the idea that a reign of virtue could be imposed from above by the insightful. Like Rousseau, the new Jacobins see politics as a choice between right and wrong. If power could be acquired by those who champion right, there is no reason, except pragmatic considerations, to respect or accommodate a diversity of views and interests. Unlike the old virtue of character, the new virtue does not aim primarily at controlling self but at controlling others. One likely avenue

---

4. In the United States, much of the contemporary hostility to a philosophical concern for historical particularity is derived from Leo Strauss, who in turn relies on German sources (e.g., Ernst Troeltsch). See, for example, Strauss, *Natural Right and History* (Chicago: University of Chicago Press, 1953), esp. 294-323. A recent example of this brand of thinking, which is sometimes simplistic and reductionistic, is Fred Baumann, "Historicism and the Constitution," in Allan Bloom, ed. *Confronting the Constitution* (Washington, D.C.: American Enterprise Institute, 1990). For a critique of the contemporary attacks on historical thinking, see Paul Gottfried, *The Search for Historical Meaning* (DeKalb: Northern Illinois University Press, 1986); and Claes G. Ryn, *Will, Imagination and Reason* (Chicago: Regnery Books, 1986), which defends historical consciousness as not only compatible with but indispensable to a defense of ethical and other universality.

for the attempted expansion of virtuous power is a vigorous presidency. Here the long-standing liberal-leftist glorification of a strong presidency to do the people's will, exemplified by a James MacGregor Burns, blends with the notion of presidential leadership advocated by a Harvey Mansfield.[5]

International adventurism is often a distraction from pressing domestic difficulties. In America today expansionism is fueled by moral-ideological passion. Allan Bloom makes clear that what he calls "the American project" is not just for Americans. "When we Americans speak seriously about politics, we mean that our principles of freedom and equality and the rights based on them are rational and everywhere applicable." World War II was for Bloom "really an educational project undertaken to force those who did not accept these principles to do so."[6] If America is the instrument of universal right, the cause of all humanity, it is easily understood that it has every reason to be diligent and insistent in imposing its will. Since the principles for which it stands are portrayed as supra-national – for Bloom they are actually opposed to national identity – nationalism may not be quite the right term for

---

5. See James MacGregor Burns, *The Deadlock of Democracy* (Englewood Cliffs, N.J.: Prentice-Hall, 1963) and Harvey Mansfield, *Taming the Prince* (New York: Free Press, 1989).

6. Bloom, *Closing*, 153.

America's missionary zeal. As America spearheads the cause of universal principles, it should presumably efface its own distinctiveness. Although countries confronted by this power are certain to see it precisely as a manifestation of nationalistic ambition, it should perhaps be regarded as nationalism only in a special sense.

But it is patriotism even less. As already explained, the patriot's pride of country is indistinguishable from moral self-restraint and a sense of the flaws of his own country. The new Jacobinism is not exactly uncritical of today's American democracy. Bloom and others complain that it is too relativistic and insufficiently faithful to the principles of its own "Founding." It should be noted, however, that since those principles are "rational and everywhere applicable" and thus monopolistic, greater dedication to American principles would increase, not reduce, the wish of Americans to dictate terms to others.

Speaking of the United States and its principles as models for all peoples is today a recurring theme in some American intellectual and political circles. Sometimes the will to power behind this refrain is barely able to keep up ideological appearances. Writes Ben Wattenberg, "It's pretty clear what the global community needs: probably a top cop, but surely a powerful global organizer. Somebody's got to do it. We're the only ones who can." Advocating a "visionary" American foreign policy, Wattenberg proclaims: "The idea of spreading democratic and American values around the world is visionary." With moralistic righteousness he adds, "It's the right thing to do." [7]

The new Jacobins are justifying a grasp for power in the midst of glaring moral, intellectual, and cultural problems in the Western world. Investing today's democracy with a world-wide moral mission signifies either a slipping hold on reality or a cynical exploitation of Western moods of escapism. The new Jacobins present their ideology as a moral response to the crisis of "liberalism" and relativism, but it is likely to hasten rather than slow the already advanced deterioration of constitutional democracy. Its abstract virtue of "principles" or "rights" bypasses the real problem of character and inspires an arrogance of power. A salutary defense of constitutional government and nationhood today would deflate, not fan, democratist ambitions. What is sorely needed is realism and frankness about the acute and life-threatening problems of Western democracy and heavy stress on the need for moral self-control and discrimination. It may be retorted that Western democracy is beyond saving and that it is too late for remedies that require a long time: that ways now have to be found to hold back chaos. Let it be said in response that, whatever the case, a reluctance of leaders to subject their ambition to ethical self-control is the source of tyranny.

---

7. Ben Wattenberg, *The Washington Times*, Aug. 8 and Aug. 1, 1990.

X

Jacobinism and Capitalism

Among the causes espoused by some of the new Jacobins is what they call "capitalism." Unfortunately, that term is as mired in philosophical confusion as "democracy." The way in which advocacy of capitalism can be an outlet for the Jacobin spirit may be explained by demonstrating that there are major moral and theoretical connections between the ideas of the French Revolution and certain modern notions of capitalism.

The French Jacobins combined a belief in abstract principles with moralistic righteousness in the effort to bestow their noble insights on all humanity. Warnings from others, including Edmund Burke, that in the reform of society concrete circumstances had to be taken into account and historical experience respected seemed to the French revolutionaries morally perverse and reactionary. No other guide was necessary than their own universal principles. To liberate mankind from oppression and enact freedom, equality, and brotherhood, a clean break with the past was necessary. Jean-Jacques Rousseau had shown the need to abandon not only old beliefs but all of the social and political structures from which they were indistinguishable. Western civilization could not be dismantled without destroying the concrete institutional and other arrangements through which it expressed itself.

The notion that all historically existing societies are full of exploitation and other evils and that a society of justice and well-being can be created only through sweeping and radical change has appeared in many versions since the time of the French Jacobins. The words "left" and "right" used to indicate the extent to which particular individuals and movements were drawn to that notion – the "left" finding it morally appealing and intellectually persuasive, the "right" finding it both morally repugnant and philosophically untenable. Today, utopian and radical sentiment of this kind is common across the political-intellectual spectrum. Indeed, some people called "conservative" are in the forefront of those who offer panaceas for the world's ills. Although these "conservatives" propose political and economic programs that appear quite different from those advocated by the conventional "left" and although they speak a different language, they sometimes share with the old "left" a belief in the salvific power and universal applicability of their programs. Even more important, the ultimate goals for society envisioned by them bear a stronger resemblance to those of the old Jacobins than might first appear.

One of the most radical expressions of the Jacobin spirit is Marxism. Since Karl Marx believes in the destruction of capitalism and the triumph of socialism, it might seem that a defender of capitalism must have little in common with Jacobinism. It is again time to insist on the need for distinctions and to point out that, like "free market" (and "democracy"), the term "capitalism" can have sharply different meanings. It should not be forgotten that among the impulses behind the French Revolution was a desire among the middle classes to be rid of various old restrictions on commerce. In today's Western society the wish for economic freedom has been taken to an extreme by various radical "libertarians." It should be carefully noted that there is a sense in which a free market would become really free only when the movement of goods and services is wholly unrestricted, unfettered not only by "external," legal or institutional checks but by the many "inner" restraints represented by the inhibitions and tastes of civilized persons. A Rousseauistic, Jacobin desire to destroy traditional ethical and cultural restraints and sociopolitical structures can thus be said to aid in the creation of a truly free market. It is not farfetched but entirely consistent to be a moral, intellectual, and cultural radical and a strong proponent of the free market—by a certain definition of the free market.

Of those in the West today who are passionate advocates of capitalism and want it introduced all over the world, many are former Marxists. The shift from being a Marxist to becoming a missionary for capitalism may be far less drastic than commonly assumed. Depending on the definition of capitalism, there can be very considerable continuity between the first and the second position.

It should be recognized, first of all, that, although Karl Marx predicted the replacement of capitalism by socialism and then by the stateless society of communism, he was a great admirer of capitalism. Like today's proponents of capitalism he credits it with unleashing enormous productive power. In the words of *The Communist Manifesto* (1848), "The bourgeoisie, during its rule of scarce one hundred years, has created more massive and more colossal productive forces than have all preceding generations together." Far from opposing the spread of capitalism, Marx believes, again like today's most enthusiastic champions of capitalism, that it must expand across the globe. It will lift mankind to a new level of development. For Marx, capitalism makes all peoples partakers of the historical progress that will finally end the suffering of mankind. "The bourgeoisie, by the rapid improvement of all instruments of production, by the immensely facilitated means of communication, draws all, even the most barbarian, nations into civilization." By "civilization" Marx here means the productive potential of modern society.[1]

The parallels between Marx and some of today's missionaries for capitalism are thus evident. An obvious difference is that Marx sees capitalism as also causing great travail and regards the revolution of the proletariat and the overthrow of capitalism as necessary for mankind's final liberation. An important question to ask about particular proponents of capitalism in the Western world today is whether they reject the doctrines of Karl Marx because of fundamental disagreements with his view of man, society, and history, or because they share much of his moral pathos and believe that the desirable society of the future is more efficiently achieved by avoiding socialism as he envisioned it. Is capitalism espoused because the revolution of the proletariat and the socialist state are seen as blind alleys, quite unnecessary for realizing an essentially egalitarian society freed of the prejudices, injustices, and constraints of traditional civilization? Is capitalism endorsed because letting it do its work is the best way of uprooting backward beliefs and related socio-political structures? Note carefully that for Marx himself one of the most important features of capitalism, as he conceives

---

1. Karl Marx and Friedrich Engels, *The Communist Manifesto* (Harmondsworth: Penguin Books, 1974), 84-85.

of it, is that it completely destroys traditional civilization, not just in the Western world, but wherever it takes hold.

A Jacobin in spirit could thus become an enthusiastic advocate of capitalism–provided it is capitalism understood in a particular way. The destruction brought by capitalism in this sense is similar to the one effected by plebiscitary democracy. In the end, the old decentralized and group-oriented society and the ethical, intellectual, and cultural beliefs that fostered it are left in ruins. It is the possibility of capitalism of this kind that created unease about the free market not just in the old Roman Catholic Church and among Christians generally but among all who wanted to preserve and develop the heritage of humane civilization.[2]

The Jacobin spirit can align itself with that set of potentialities in capitalism that are most destructive of the ways of traditional society. It seizes upon and gives wider circulation to vague, nice-sounding, but sophistical notions like "equality of economic opportunity," "equality at the starting line," or "a level playing field." Because most people, especially in the United States, spontaneously oppose obstacles to opportunity

---

2. For examples of official Roman Catholic concern about the moral dangers of capitalism before the Church was influenced by a socialistic view of capitalism, see the Papal encyclicals *Rerum Novarum* (1891) and *Quadragesimo Anno* (1931).

that are unreasonable, irrelevant to tasks to be performed, or otherwise artificial, it is easily overlooked that, if taken quite seriously and literally, equality of economic opportunity requires a radical transformation of society. It requires the removal of all those considerations which, in traditional civilization, limit and structure economic activity so as to make it compatible with or supportive of humane values that lie beyond supply and demand. Equality of opportunity, taken literally, means treating all persons—moral and immoral, noble and ignoble, crude and refined—equally as long as they can be expected to perform adequately by some narrowly economic, utilitarian standard. Other types of criteria should be set aside.

But civilization depends on *not* letting purely economic considerations dominate society. The logic of equality of opportunity is to drive out extra-economic standards, to remove premiums and penalties that nudge or force individuals to be people of one kind rather than another. A couple of random examples may suggest the practical consequences of carrying equality of economic opportunity to its ultimate conclusion. The tax codes of all countries favor and disfavor some social arrangements. This is to slant economic opportunity, to make it unequal. Real equality would require, for instance, that families and homeowners should have no tax benefits not available to all others, including young singles and those uninterested in the rootedness of home ownership. In business, decisions to hire and promote should not favor the responsible, courteous, well-groomed individual over the slick, ill-mannered, sloppy person except insofar as the difference might affect productivity. In professional sports, the personally odious player should have the same chance to play and make money as the one who sets an example for others, as long as his professional skills are comparable. The list of needed changes could be extended indefinitely until society is drained of every civilized preference and civilization ceases to exist.

The phrase "a level playing field" as a description of capitalism (or democracy) may seem rather innocuous. As loosely used by some, it can mean simply that no one should have an unfair advantage over another. People of privileged position should not be able to deny others the advancement and the rewards to which they are entitled by natural ability and hard work. Clearly, a soundly traditional society needs counterweights to social in-breeding, stagnation, and snobbery. All societies need the revivification of institutions and behavior that comes from challenges to old ways. Balancing the need for continuity and the need for change is the great task of civilization. But what is unfair advantage? Civilization attempts to enact its preferences precisely by giving advantages and encouragement to some, namely to those who come closest to embodying the values that are central to civilization, and placing obstacles in the way of others, namely of those who deliberately and egregiously threaten those values. Except in a special, limited sense, civilization does not aim to treat people equally. Doing so would be unjust, for no two individuals are the same. The aim of civilization is to structure life so that, to the greatest extent possible, those who enjoy or acquire advantages and influence are also, by the highest standards, deserving of them. What is appealing to the Jacobin about "the level playing field" is that it suggests the absence of traditional socio-political patterns that encourage some types of behavior and discourage others. As used by the modern Jacobin, the phrase speaks of a society swept free of the historically evolved discriminations between high and low through which civilization defines, manifests, and preserves itself.

Ensuring real equality of economic opportunity by these standards would obviously require much interference with the economy as it exists in actual societies. Taken literally and seriously, the mentioned notions of equality of opportunity must, in practice, result in great expansion of the administrative state and in the eventual blending of capitalism and socialism. If "equality at the starting-line" is assumed actually to mean what it says, capitalism requires, among other things, the abolition of inheritance, which gives the children of the well-to-do an advantage over others. A certain kind of advocacy of capitalism turns out to have much in common with the Jacobin passion for an egalitarian, homogeneous society.

But capitalism, or the free market, can be understood in a very different manner. It is possible to distinguish between different forms of the free economy along lines similar to the distinction between constitutional and plebiscitary democracy. A free market of goods and services may exist in a decentralized, group-oriented society in which the outlook and behavior of individuals and firms are leavened by ethical and other discipline and in which both supply and demand are structured by corresponding civilized desires. In this economy relations between competitors may be softened by mutual respect and consideration. A free market of this type would share in the ethos characteristic also of constitutional government. It would be an integral part of the civilized society with its institutionally expressed likes and dislikes.

The vital importance of the social setting of the market is stressed by the economist Wilhelm Röpke. "The market economy is one thing in a society where atomization, mass, proletarianization, and concentration rule," in which moral rootlessness robs competition of traditional ethical restraints, and in which producers cater indiscriminately to consumer demand. The market is quite another thing, Röpke insists, in the kind of decentralized, group-centered society that was described earlier as fostering the character on which constitutionalism depends. "In such a society," Röpke writes, "wealth would be widely dispersed; people's lives would have solid foundations; genuine communities, from the family upward, would form a background of moral support for the individual; there would be counterweights to competition and the mechanical operation of prices; people would have roots and would not be adrift in life without anchor." [3]

What should be understood is that the distinction here developed is not between slightly different versions of one and the same economic system but between opposed potentialities that are no more compatible than are constitutional and plebiscitary democracy.

Critics of capitalism typically identify it with its worst possibilities: ruthless competition, exploitation, greed, crude commercialism, social atomism, etc. These are said to be of the very essence of a free economy. In reality, the prominence of such phenomena is a sign that capitalism is operating within a society in which people lack ethical, aesthetical, and other inhibitions and strong communal ties, a society in which institutional structures do not embody civilized purposes and in which neither supply nor demand recognizes any higher standards. Critics of democracy similarly identify democracy with its worst potentialities: unchecked majoritarianism, political irresponsibility, demagoguery, rule by pandering to the lowest common denominator, etc. Here, too, the alleged essence of the phenomenon in question is how it performs in a society where

---

3. Wilhelm Röpke, *A Humane Economy* (Indianapolis: Liberty Press, 1971), 35.

civilized restraints are weak. Both points of view are unhistorical and reductionistic. In reality, capitalism and democracy have no single definition or "essence." They exist only in particular historical manifestations. These can be sharply different depending on the ethical and cultural health of the particular societies in which they operate. They can be compatible with the ends of the good society, in which case their institutions and practices are integral to the structures and practices of civilization. But they can also be destructive of higher values, in which case they manifest the structures and practices of the deteriorating society.

The social setting of an acceptable free economy has been described by Röpke in a way that shows its connection with what was earlier explained as the ethical and cultural context of constitutional popular government.

> Self-discipline, a sense of justice, honesty, fairness, chivalry, moderation, public spirit, respect for human dignity, firm ethical norms – all of these are things which people must posses before they go to market and compete with each other. These are the indispensable supports which preserve both market and competition from degeneration. Family, church, genuine communities, and tradition are their sources. It is also necessary that people should grow up in conditions which favor such moral convictions, conditions of a natural order, conditions promoting co-operation, respecting tradition, and giving moral support to the individual. . . . It is the foundation upon which the ethics of the market economy must rest. It is an order which fosters individual independence and responsibility as much as the

public spirit which connects the individual with the community and limits his greed.[4]

It has been argued here that constitutional democracy has demanding ethical and cultural prerequisites and that it is not easily created and maintained. In a morally and culturally deteriorating society it threatens to transform itself into a plebiscitary regime. This will begin to give democracy a bad name among people with discriminating standards. A similar argument can be made with regard to the free market. If the latter ceases to exhibit the discipline and responsibility characteristic of a civilized society, it will, even if it continues to produce goods and services, begin to give the free market a bad reputation among people who look beyond quantitative standards.

When the Roman Catholic Church expressed reservations about the free market, these were, in the final analysis, concerns about more general developments in Western civilization. Warnings about the possible dangers of the free economy could have been directed against parallel dangers posed by other social freedoms, and by popular government. The dangers did not inhere in the free market "as such," for no such thing can exist. They inhered in the free market in a

---

4. *Ibid.*, 125. For a brief but philosophically lucid and incisive discussion of the relationship between ethics and economics, see Joseph Baldacchino, *Economics and the Moral Order* (Washington, D.C.: National Humanities Institute, 1985).

particular historical period marked by shaky moral and other standards.

As aligned with and shaped by a spirit of radicalism, capitalism can do much to obliterate traditional ethical and cultural standards and uproot traditional communities. For some of today's proponents of capitalism one of its appeals may be precisely that it can accomplish a task of destruction. Praise for capitalism can be, among other things, an outlet for resentment against traditional elites and a desire to sweep from positions of influence people seen as upholding old-fashioned, more aristocratic standards. Simultaneous advocacy of capitalism and majoritarian democracy reinforces and broadens the attack upon the old society. As adjusted to changing historical circumstances, the spirit of Rousseau and Marx can here find plentiful new opportunities.

That so much of today's discussion about capitalism, democracy, and related subjects ignores or glosses over distinctions of fundamental importance is a source of major intellectual and practical confusion. Sound and unsound ideas, destructive and constructive, are mixed in sometimes very odd combinations. Some rather curious intellectual and political alliances are formed. Were it not for the dominant underlying trend and the lack of philosophical discipline, this theoretical and practical commotion might seem a promising opportunity for a badly needed intellectual and cultural reconstitution and realignment.

But ideological passion drives out or discourages serious thought as well as deeper sensibility. It is indicative of the influence of the Jacobin spirit in the Western world that a fondness for abstract general schemes and utopian visions should today have attraction even for people said to be "conservative" or on "the right." This development says a great deal about the scope and depth of the Western flight from reality.

XI

Recovering Moral Realism

What has here been called the new Jacobinism refers less to particular individuals than to a general tendency within today's Western society. It does of course shape the mind and the imagination of people in varying degrees. Among those who give ardent expression to it, there are some who simultaneously hold rather different and more realistic beliefs. Failure to make distinctions between incompatible ideas is a dangerous feature of intellectual and political discussion. All too frequently, utopian-ideological passion creates a false sense of consistency. Whether the new Jacobinism pulls particular individuals in a predominantly rationalistic or sentimental direction, it distracts the person from uncomfortable truths about self and society.

The willingness of the Western democracies to look away from pressing and dangerous problems is ominous. So is the hostility with which those who dominate public opinion usually greet attempts really to confront those problems and deal with them in depth. The Western democracies are more receptive to various pretentious socio-political proposals inspired by abstract and sentimental "virtue." But these schemes do more to aggravate than alleviate the problems. Only superficially does their espousal of "moral values" address the needs of a morally fragmenting society. They exacerbate the flight from individual responsibility while indulging the will to power of those who champion them.

The moral and political panaceas and illusions that hold such appeal in today's Western societies invite a neglect or postponement of more concrete and immediate personal obligations. For a genuine recovery of Western society to be possible, the addictive habits of moral escapism and conceit will have to be broken. The heart of the matter is the urgent need for a reawakened awareness of personal character and responsibility as the basis of the civilized society. The individual must be encouraged to face the hard and primary obligations of the here and now, chief of which is improvement of self and doing right by "neighbor." Social and political arrangements can assume humane and constructive form only if they evolve from individual lives that are soundly ordered. From a new moral realism of this kind and from a corresponding strengthening of character can emerge a reconstituted sense of proportion and priorities and a more sober assessment of what can be achieved through politics.

It must not be denied that in the civilized society government has large and important functions that cannot be satisfactorily performed by another authority. Some of these functions are inherently centralized or are not easily decentralized. But much of the accumulation and centralization of power in today's Western democracies is derived from false or faulty definitions of problems and from pleasing but pernicious belief in abstract and distant solutions. A new willingness to confront the problems of life personally and up close so that individual action and initiative are morally reinvigorated would bolster private and local community. It would also tend to bring the handling of social and political matters closer to those who are most directly affected and most alert to specific needs and opportunities. A reaffirmation of real personal responsibility would not only limit and decentralize power but make it less arrogant and heavy-handed.

It might be commented that it is not realistic to expect the Western democracies to sober up morally in this manner. If indeed it is not realistic, one can only expect the final demise of constitutional democracy. What replaces it will bear little or no resemblance to the Rousseauistic dream of plebiscitary rule.

Index

Abortions, 59
Abstract moralism, 67-73
AIDS, 59
Aristotle: misinterpreted as democratist, 68; 25
Arts: decline of, 59
Autonomous groups, 21

Babbitt, Irving, 39n1
Baldacchino, Joseph, 89n4
Baumann, Fred, 72n4
Bloom, Allan: agrees with Rousseau, 69-70; and French Revolution, 68; and new Jacobinism, 68-74: contrasted with Burke, 68; on American democracy, 74; quoted on World War II, 73; quoted, 68, 69-70; 68-74
Blum, Carol, 42n4
Burke, Edmund: contrasted with Bloom, 68-69; quoted on need for change, 16; 77
Burns, James MacGregor, 73

Capitalism: and aristocratic restraints, 90; and majoritarian democracy, 90; and traditional morality, 86-89; different meanings, 23, 79-90; importance of social setting, 87-90
Catholic Church, Roman: and capitalism, 82, 89
Centralization of power: and social fragmentation, 64
Christians: and capitalism, 82
Churches: and sentimentalism, 59-60
Citizens (Schama), 13n1
Closing of the American Mind, The (Bloom), 69n1, 70n2, 73n6
Communist Manifesto, The (Marx and Engels), 80, 81n1
Confronting the Constitution (Bloom, ed.), 72n4
Conservative Constitution, The (Kirk), 35n2
Constitutional democracy: and aristocratic restraints, 33-34; and autonomous groups, 21-22; assumes decentralized society, 21-22; assumes flawed human nature, 20-21; fosters peace, 47; opposed by Rousseau, 40; 19-23
Constitution, U.S.: opposed to plebiscitary democracy, 33-34; 56

97

Cosmopolitanism:
  compatible with patriotism, 45-47
Crime, 58

Deadlock of Democracy, The (Burns), 73n5
Decadence, 60
Decentralized society:
  roots in Christianity, 25
Democracy and the Ethical Life (Ryn), 19n1, 39n1
Democracy, constitutional: and egalitarianism, 40; and human nature, 21; fosters peace, 47; opposed by Rousseau, 40-41; 19-23
Democracy in America (de Tocqueville), 66n5
Democracy, majoritarian or plebiscitary: and egalitarianism, 40; and human nature, 21; conflicts with freedom, 52; favors centralization, 22-23; leads to thought control, 65-66; opposed by Framers, 35; Rousseau on, 40-42; threatens peace, 47; 19-23
Democracy, representative: fosters peace, 74; opposed by Rousseau, 40-41; 19-23
Democracy: and peace, 47; and personal responsibility, 11-12; decline of, 9-10, 55-66; importance of social setting, 87-88; two kinds, 10, 19-23
Discourse on Political Economy, A (Rousseau), 43n6
Drug abuse, 58

E pluribus unum, 52
Economics and the Moral Order (Baldacchino), 89n4
Egalitarianism: inimical to diversity and pluralism, 69-73; 40
Electoral College, 34, 56
Enlightened self-interest: insufficiency of, 61
Entertainment, 59
"Equality of economic opportunity": criticized, 82-85; leads to socialism, 85
Ethical universality: and freedom, 52; and pluralism, 52; compatible with history, 49-51; harmonizes diversity, 51-52
Federalist No. 10:
  quoted, 33-34
Federalist Papers, The (Hamilton, Madison,

Jay), 34n1
Fragmentation, social: and centralization of power, 64; 62-64
Framers of U.S. Constitution: misinterpretations of, 68, 69-71; opposed plebiscitary rule, 35; 52
Free market: and morality, 29; different meanings, 23; 79-90
French Jacobins, 66, 77-79
French Revolution, 12-13, 17-18, 79

General will (Rousseau), 41-42
Gottfried, Paul, 72n4
Government: dependent upon culture, 36-37; role in civilized society, 95
Government of Poland, The (Rousseau), 43n7

Hamilton, Alexander, 34n1
Hartz, Louis: quoted on Locke, 70; 70n3
Historical thinking: compatible with universal morality, 71-72, 72n4
"Historicism and the Constitution" (Baumann), 72n4

Humane Economy, A (Röpke), 87n3, 89n4
Inflation, 59
Internationalist ideology: and centralization of government, 64, 67-69

Jacobin clubs, 12-13
Jacobin Clubs in the French Revolution, The (Kennedy), 13n1
Jacobin spirit, 18
Jacobinism, new: and Bloom, 68-74; and "conservatives," 78-79, 91; as general tendency, 93-94; 13-15
Jacobins, French, 12-13, 42, 66, 77-79
Jacobins, new: and "capitalism," 77-95; and international adventurism, 73-75; Rousseau's influence on, 42; potential for tyranny, 71-72; 67-75
Jay, John, 34n1
Jefferson, Thomas, 71

Kennedy, Michael, 13n1
Kirk, Russell, 35n2

Lawlessness, 58
"Level playing field": criticized, 82-85; leads to socialism, 85
Liberal Tradition in

America, The (Hartz), 70n3
Libertarians, 79
Liberty: different meanings, 23
Locke, John, 68

Madison, James, 34n1
Majoritarian democracy: and egalitarianism, 40; and human nature, 21; conflicts with freedom, 52; favors centralization, 22-23; leads to thought control, 65-66; opposed by Framers, 35; Rousseau on, 40-42
Mansfield, Harvey, 73
Marx, Karl: quoted on capitalism, 80, 80-81; 79, 80, 90
Marxism, 79-82
McDonald, Forrest, 35n2
Modernity: opposed potentialities of, 17-18
Moral abstractionism, 67-73
Moral self-control: disappearance from Western society, 55-56
Moral virtue, traditional: and international relations, 27-28; 25-27, 31-32
Morality, sentimental: shirks personal responsibility, 26; supports dictatorial government and imperialism, 28
Morality, universal: compatible with historical thinking, 71-72, 72n4
Morality: and the free market, 29

Nationalism: and abstract rights, 73-74; distinguished from patriotism, 45-47
New Jacobinism, the: as general tendency, 93-94; and "conservatives," 78-79, 91; and Bloom, 68-74
New Jacobins, the: and "capitalism," 77-95; and international adventurism, 73-75; potential for tyranny, 71-72; 67-75
Nisbet, Robert: on autonomous groups, 21-22; on centralization, 64, 64n4

"One-man-one-vote," 40

Paine, Thomas, 71
Patriotism: compatible with cosmopolitanism, 45-47; distinguished from nationalism, 45-47
Plato: and democracy, 31-32; misinterpreted

as democratist, 68; on democracy, 65, 66; quoted on the decadent society, 60; quoted on democracy and crime, 58; 58n1, 60n2
Plebiscitary democracy: and egalitarianism, 40; and human nature, 21; conflicts with freedom, 52; favors centralization, 22-23; leads to thought control, 65-66; opposed by Framers, 35; Rousseau on, 40-42
Politics: as civil war by non-violent means, 60-61
Power: centralization of, 57-58
Principles: abstract: promote international adventurism, 73-75; 71

Röpke, Wilhelm: quoted on social setting of the market, 86-87; 88-89
Religion: and sentimentalism, 59-60
Representative democracy: and aristocratic restraints, 33-34; and autonomous groups, 21-22; assumes decentralized society, 21-22; assumes flawed human nature, 20-21; fosters peace, 47; opposed by Rousseau, 40; 19-23
Rights: abstract: promote international adventurism, 73-75; 71
Robespierre, Maximilien de: Rousseau's influence on, 42
Roman Catholic Church: and capitalism, 82, 89
Rousseau, Jean-Jacques: advocates dismantling of Western civilization, 78; and French Revolution, 12-13; and militarism, 42; and nationalism, 42-43; and plebiscitary democracy, 20; favors centralization, 40-41; his radical redefinition of moral virtue, 12; opposes self-restraint, 39-40; quoted, 40, 42, 42-43, 43; 40n2, 43n6, 43n7, 43n8, 52, 69, 72, 90
Ryn, Claes G., 19n1, 39n1, 42n4, 42n5, 69n1, 72n4

Schama, Simon, 13n1
Self-indulgence: leads to centralization of power, 57-58
Self-interest, enlightened: insufficiency of, 61

Senate, U.S.: direct popular election of, 56
Sentimental morality: shirks personal responsibility, 26; supports dictatorial government and imperialism, 28
Sentimentalism: and religion, 59-60
Sexual promiscuity, 58-59
Social fragmentation: and centralization of power, 64; 62-64
Sparta, 42
Strauss, Leo, 72n4
Supreme Court, U.S., 34, 57

Tocqueville, Alexis de: quoted on "soft" democratic despotism, 66
Traditional moral virtue: and international relations, 25-28; 31-32
Traditionalism: not mere return to past, 15-17
Troelsch, Ernst, 72n4

Uniformity, 42

Universal morality: compatible with historical thinking, 71-72, 72n4
Universal good: realized through particular actions, 50-51
"Universality or Uniformity?" (Ryn), 69n1
Universality, ethical: and freedom, 52; and pluralism, 52; compatible with history, 49-51; harmonizes diversity, 51-52

Virtuous power: Rousseau's notion of, 42

Wattenberg, Ben: quoted on spreading democracy, 74-75
Western tradition: has flaws, 18; spurious interpretations of, 68
Will, general (Rousseau), 41-42
World War II: Bloom's view of, 73